A House for Snail

written by
Vivian French

illustrated by
Ivan Mitrevski

CAMBRIDGE
UNIVERSITY PRESS

UCL
Institute of Education

Snail was looking for a house.

'Where do you live, Worm?' said Snail.

'I live here in the earth,' said Worm.

4

'Can I live here, too?' said Snail.

'No,' said Worm. 'You can't wriggle under the ground.'

'Where do you live, Butterfly?' said Snail.

'I live here in the flowers,' said Butterfly.

'Can I live here, too?' said Snail.

'No,' said Butterfly. 'You can't fly like me.'

Snail met a spider.

'Do you live here?' he said.

'Yes, I live in a web,' said Spider.

'Can I live here, too?' said Snail.

'No,' said Spider. 'You're too heavy.'

Snail met a bee.

'Do you live here?' he said.

'Yes, I live in a hive with all my friends,' said Bee.

10

'Can I live here too?' said Snail.

'No,' said Bee. 'You're too big.'

'Snail,' said Bee. 'Why are you looking for a house?'

'I want to be safe and warm,' said Snail.

'But Snail,' said Bee, 'You've got a house on your back!'

'Oh!' said Snail. 'So I have!'
And he went inside.

14

'Wow!' said Snail. 'My house is just right for me! I can live here!'

A House for Snail · Vivian French

Teaching notes written by Sue Bodman and Glen Franklin

Using this book

Developing reading comprehension

Snail looks for a house, only to find that he has been carrying the ideal home on his back all the time. The search is told through a repetitive structure with lots of opportunities for developing reading with phrasing as the characters interact. This learning objective is best supported by encouraging children to follow the print with their eyes, only rarely using finger-pointing at points of difficulty.

Grammar and sentence structure

- Some repetition of phrase patterns, but with more variation of sentence structure evident.
- Fully punctuated question and answer structure.
- Familiar oral language structures with some literary language.

Word meaning and spelling

- Opportunity to rehearse a wide range of known high frequency words.
- Practise and consolidation of reading regular decodable words.

Curriculum links

Science and Nature – Animals make their homes in many different places. In this book, Snail finds out that he is not suited to a home in a web, in a hive or under the ground. This book links to finding out about animal habitats.

Learning outcomes

Children can:

- use punctuation to inform phrasing and expression
- use phonic knowledge to solve new and novel words
- comment on the events and characters in the story, making links to other stories.

A guided reading lesson

Book Introduction

Give each child a book and read the title to them.

Orientation

Give a brief overview of the book, using the verb in the same form as it is in text.

Snail was looking for a house. He asked lots of animals if he could share their home. Let's see if he can find a home.

Ask the children to read the title for themselves.

Preparation

Page 2: Ask the children to identify the animals and animal homes that they can see in the picture. Draw out the vocabulary, supporting where necessary. Ask the children to think about whether the homes would be good for Snail – why/why not?

Page 4: *Snail asks a question.* Point to the question mark. *See this question mark? It means we have to read it in a certain way.* Model reading a question. Ask the children to find another example of a question on page 5 and ask them to rehearse reading it with the correct intonation. Repeat the rehearsal of questions on page 6 and 7 if necessary.